FOURSQUARE ————————— ✝ 🕊 🍷 👑

21 Days of Prayer + Fasting 2024

Praying
the
Word

January 8-28, 2024

What's Inside?

Praying the Word in 2024

Thank you for joining us for 21 Days of Prayer + Fasting 2024! This annual time of dedicated prayer, which is produced by The U.S. Foursquare Church, is now used by Foursquare churches and missionary workers around the world. As you pray each day, from Jan. 8-28, know that you are praying together with a global community of many tribes and tongues.

This year we will be "Praying the Word." Each day you will be encouraged as you pray through Scripture and are guided through times of prayer and reflection. If it's helpful for your prayer journey, you can purchase a book on Amazon, or sign up for daily email reminders at FoursquarePrayer.org.

For those who choose to fast over the next three weeks, you may abstain as it seems good to you and the Lord. Pray about it. Perhaps you are being called to give up a specific food, some sort of technology or another habit. We know the Lord will bless your fasting practice, and we pray you are blessed during this time of sacrifice.

Visit FoursquarePrayer.org to find resources on fasting and praying, and to download the **Family Moments** daily guide. That's right: You can walk through these 21 Days of Prayer + Fasting together with kiddo-friendly activities and prayers. There's something for every member of the family inside.

You are free to reproduce this 21 Days of Prayer + Fasting guide, available in English and in Spanish, but it should be distributed at no cost. Visit FoursquarePrayer.org to find tons of helpful resources as you communicate and gather your church or community around prayer.

Thank you again for making intentional time to pray in 2024. We can't wait to see how God uses this time.

—The U.S. Foursquare Church

También disponible en español

¡Descargue o compre una copia de los 21 Días de Ayuno + Oración 2024 en español! Inscríbase para recibir correos electrónicos y encuentre recursos para su iglesia también. Visite OracionCuadrangular.org.

God is God, without rival or *equal*, and we offer Him our thanks and praise. Our *highest aim* is to know and love Him with everything within us.

Days 01 through **03**

Day 01 —— Offering praise

Shift your mind into a place of worship, seeing God's majesty and praising Him for all He has done.

Today's Scripture

"Among the gods there is none like You, Lord; no deeds can compare with Yours. All the nations You have made will come and worship before You, Lord; they will bring glory to Your name. For You are great and do marvelous deeds; You alone are God. Teach me Your way, Lord, that I may rely on Your faithfulness; give me an undivided heart, that I may fear Your name. I will praise You, Lord my God, with all my heart; I will glorify Your name forever."
—Psalm 86:8-12 (NIV)

"Blessed be Your glorious name, and may it be exalted above all blessing and praise. You alone are the Lord. You made the heavens, even the highest heavens, and all their starry host, the earth and all that is on it, the seas and all that is in them. You give life to everything, and the multitudes of heaven worship You."
—Nehemiah 9:5-6 (NIV)

Additional Scripture
Psalm 139:13-18 (NKJV)

Reflect on the Word

Let's begin our collective 21 Days of Prayer + Fasting by looking up and seeing Jesus, high and lifted up, eternally enthroned over all creation. As ministers, a vocational hazard we sometimes face is losing sight of God's majesty and wonder just as we are trying to present Him as majestic and wondrous to others! Prayer and praise go hand in hand to totally renew our souls. He is worthy of our praise. Let's pray together.

Prayer + Contemplation

1. Take time right now to recapture the glory and awe of God in whatever way feels right (singing, prayer, etc.).

2. Ask the Holy Spirit to bring to mind areas in your life where God has become tame or small, and allow Him to expand in your heart.

3. Go for a walk in a quiet and beautiful setting, or drive somewhere peaceful. Pause in a safe place to look up at the sky, and allow creation to lead your heart into praise and worship for all God is and what He has done.

Family Moment : ABCs of praise

Read Psalm 86:10. You just read a prayer of praise! When we praise God, we declare truths about who He is. Can you think of words that describe God? Create your family's ABCs of praise. Starting with each letter of the alphabet, allow family members to write down or share aloud a word that describes God. Continue your way through the alphabet, celebrating your ABCs of praise when you arrive at letter Z!

Notes

Day 02 —— Expressing gratitude

Remember who God is and what He has done, and let us praise His holy name.

Today's Scripture

"Oh come, let us sing to the Lord! Let us shout joyfully to the Rock of our salvation. Let us come before His presence with thanksgiving; let us shout joyfully to Him with psalms. For the Lord is the great God, and the great King above all gods. In His hand are the deep places of the earth; the heights of the hills are His also. The sea is His, for He made it; and His hands formed the dry land. Oh come, let us worship and bow down; let us kneel before the Lord our Maker. For He is our God, and we are the people of His pasture, and the sheep of His hand."
—Psalm 95:1-7 (NKJV)

"Praise the Lord, my soul; all my inmost being, praise His holy name. Praise the Lord, my soul, and forget not all His benefits—who forgives all your sins and heals all your diseases, who redeems your life from the pit and crowns you with love and compassion, who satisfies your desires with good things so that your youth is renewed like the eagle's."
—Psalm 103:1-5 (NIV)

Reflect on the Word

We often remember the things we should forget, and forget what we should remember. One of the central roles of prayer is to reorient our hearts toward gratitude and thankfulness to Christ. G.K. Chesterton wrote that "gratitude is happiness doubled by wonder." These scriptures help us meditate on the wonder of God's creation and remember His infinite goodness. May the Spirit awaken our hearts in gratitude as we reflect on His Word!

Prayer + Contemplation

1. In the Notes section of this guide or in your journal, write down anything that comes to your mind throughout the day that is cause for expressing thanks to God. At the end the day, review your list and give your heavenly Father your gratitude.

2. When you go for a walk or take a drive today, instead of listening to a podcast, turn on some praise music and crank up the volume louder than you normally would. Let everything within you give thanks to God!

3. The apostle Paul encouraged us to "give thanks in all circumstances" (1 Thess. 5:18, NIV). That means even the difficult things we face. Take a moment to thank God for the hard things you're going through, and trust that He will use them for His glory.

Family Moment: Seeds of gratitude

Read Psalm 103:1-5. Why do you think it's important for us to give thanks to God, even for things that might seem ordinary? Make a top 10 list of things you are each thankful for. Share your lists with one another aloud, and thank God together for each thing, no matter how small. Post the list on the fridge or somewhere you can see it, and add one more thing you are grateful for each day this week.

Notes

_____

_____

_____

_____

_____

_____

_____

_____

_____

_____

_____

_____

_____

_____

_____

_____

_____

_____

Day 03 — Seeking His presence

Prayer and fasting are surefire ways to bring us back into God's holy presence. Be still in Him.

Today's Scripture

"One thing I ask from the Lord, this only do I seek: that I may dwell in the house of the Lord all the days of my life, to gaze on the beauty of the Lord and to seek Him in His temple."
—Psalm 27:4 (NIV)

"I want to know Christ—yes, to know the power of His resurrection and participation in His sufferings, becoming like Him in his death, and so, somehow, attaining to the resurrection from the dead. Not that I have already obtained all this, or have already arrived at my goal, but I press on to take hold of that for which Christ Jesus took hold of me. Brothers and sisters, I do not consider myself yet to have taken hold of it. But one thing I do: Forgetting what is behind and straining toward what is ahead, I press on toward the goal to win the prize for which God has called me heavenward in Christ Jesus."
—Philippians 3:10-14 (NIV)

Reflect on the Word

When we look at Scripture, we don't see stories of morally superior heroes and faultless churches; what we find again and again are people who set their hearts on seeking after God. Even the holiest saint needs to enter God's presence to keep their faith and love for Him from growing cold. Prayer and fasting are a way to accomplish this. Through our actions, Jesus stirs up and renews our love and longing for Him.

Prayer + Contemplation

1. We live in a world with endless counterfeit options for what can "fill" us, but often what we think will guide us merely distracts us. Pray for God to fill your soul to the brim with His goodness.

2. As you fast in the way that is best for you, pray that God will fill the void left by whatever you have cut out and that your love for Him will grow.

3. Take time right now to pause and wait on the Lord. Open yourself to Him and be content in silence. As you pray, welcome His transforming Spirit.

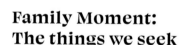

Family Moment: The things we seek

Read Psalm 27:4. What does it mean to "seek"? The Bible shows us that seeking is what we think about, the things we love and where we spend our time. God knows our lives are filled with lots of distractions. Thankfully, followers of Jesus have the Holy Spirit as guide and helper. Make and decorate a "telescope" out of a paper-towel tube, and write the words from Psalm 27:4 on the tube. Play a game of I Spy and "seek" things while only looking through the telescope. Adults, now guide kids toward finding things like the Bible, the nature God created or framed Scripture. See how much easier it is to seek and find when you have guidance? That's what the Holy Spirit does for us every day!

Notes

_____

_____

_____

_____

_____

_____

_____

_____

_____

_____

_____

_____

_____

_____

_____

_____

_____

_____

_____

Humbled in His *presence,* we posture ourselves before God so that He cleanses, *changes* and redirects us.

Days *04* through *06*

Day 04 —— True repentance

Above all else, we desire to walk with God with clean hands, a pure heart and true repentance.

Today's Scripture

"Have mercy upon me, O God, according to Your lovingkindness; according to the multitude of Your tender mercies, blot out my transgressions. Wash me thoroughly from my iniquity, and cleanse me from my sin."
—Psalm 51:1-2 (NKJV)

"Create in me a clean heart, O God, and renew a steadfast spirit within me. Do not cast me away from Your presence, and do not take Your Holy Spirit from me. Restore to me the joy of Your salvation, and uphold me by Your generous Spirit."
—Psalm 51:10-12 (NKJV)

Additional Scripture
1 John 1:7-9 (NIV)
Psalm 51:10-17 (NKJV)

Prayer + Contemplation

1. Take time and reflect on the nature and condition of your heart. Where have you grown weary? Where have you allowed sin a foothold? Where has your heart become hard or numb? Confess, repent and allow forgiveness to begin to restore your heart.

2. Make a list of pastors and leaders around you, and pray for God to protect and restore Himself as their first love.

3. Pray that God would pour out His Spirit upon our church communities and reveal any repentance He desires from us.

Reflect on the Word

As we contend for the gospel, our hearts can become weary and hardened in the struggles of life. Today, let's posture our hearts in repentance as we long to align ourselves rightly as followers of Jesus. In this hour, we believe that the church must return to a first love for Jesus, marked by a genuine fear of the Lord. Above all else, we desire to walk with God with clean hands, a pure heart and true repentance wherever we have allowed our hearts to become calloused. As we do this, may we stand in the forgiveness and transformation of Jesus.

Family Moment: Clean hearts

Read 1 John 1:7-9. What does it mean to repent? It's when we turn away from our sin and turn toward God. God loves us so much that when we confess our sins, He is faithful to forgive! Adults, now is a great time to share an example of messing up and seeking forgiveness. Distribute paper and coloring supplies, and have everyone draw a heart. Ask the Holy Spirit, "Is there any sin in my heart for which I need to repent?" Give family members time to respond with words or drawings before regrouping and celebrating God's faithful forgiveness!

Notes

_____

_____

_____

_____

_____

_____

_____

_____

_____

_____

_____

_____

_____

_____

_____

_____

_____

Day 05 —— Transparency and trust

Living out a ministry calling requires total trust in the Lord and reliance on Him.

Today's Scripture

"How long, Lord? Will You forget me forever? How long will You hide Your face from me? How long must I wrestle with my thoughts and day after day have sorrow in my heart? How long will my enemy triumph over me? Look on me and answer, Lord my God. Give light to my eyes, or I will sleep in death and my enemy will say, 'I have overcome him,' and my foes will rejoice when I fall. But I trust in Your unfailing love; my heart rejoices in Your salvation. I will sing the Lord's praise, for He has been good to me."
—Psalm 13:1-6 (NIV)

Additional Scripture
Proverbs 3:5-6 (NIV)

Reflect on the Word

Ministry is costly. Our challenges may differ, but the struggle of leadership is something we all share. Without transparency before God and trusted community, we can often allow these challenges to move us away from hope and faith in God. Today we are praying about the hardships we are experiencing and confessing any places that we must restore trust in the Lord. As leaders, we must fight to live honest and transparent lives, and put on display the faithfulness and goodness of God as He meets us in our needs.

Prayer + Contemplation

1. Take time and reflect on the challenges you are facing. As you name them, begin to pray into every situation for the courage to stand in faith and trust. Where you need help, take this transparency, and invite in a trusted ally. Remind yourself of the God who delivers, and take courage in His promises.

2. Pray for the challenges you know that other leaders around you are facing. Pray for God's intervention, that He would cover them in His grace as they contend.

3. Pray for the challenges facing the church both nationally and internationally. Ask God for an impartation of faith over the church so we will trust Him as we lead into the future.

Family Moment: Trust walk

Read Proverbs 3:5-6. Construct a simple obstacle course in your home. Take turns navigating the course with one person blindfolded and another person guiding. Gather back together for discussion. How

did it feel to trust someone to get you through the course? Read Proverbs 3:5-6 again. How do we know we can trust God? He always keeps His promises! Share with your children some examples of when you trusted God in the past. When is it hard to trust God? Pray for one another, trusting in a God who always keeps His promises.

Notes

Day 06 —— Walk worthy

God has placed a calling on each of our lives; let's choose to live lives worthy of Him.

Today's Scripture

"For this reason we also, since the day we heard it, do not cease to pray for you, and to ask that you may be filled with the knowledge of His will in all wisdom and spiritual understanding; that you may walk worthy of the Lord, fully pleasing Him, being fruitful in every good work and increasing in the knowledge of God; strengthened with all might, according to His glorious power, for all patience and longsuffering with joy; giving thanks to the Father who has qualified us to be partakers of the inheritance of the saints in the light. He has delivered us from the power of darkness and conveyed us into the kingdom of the Son of His love, in whom we have redemption through His blood, the forgiveness of sins."
—Colossians 1:9-14 (NKJV)

Additional Scripture
Matt. 6:12-15 (NIV)

Reflect on the Word

Jesus has invited us into His greatest desire: that the world would be reconciled back to God. We have been filled with the Spirit, anointed for our generation and commissioned to see the kingdom of God on Earth as it is in heaven. Considering all that God has done, we desire to live lives worthy of Him. Let's reclaim the privilege of belonging to Jesus and put the radical love of God on display in all that we do.

Prayer + Contemplation

1. Take time and reflect on the moments of calling and purpose that mark your life. Why are you leading? What has God spoken to over the years? What are the prophetic words that have marked your journey? Take hold again of the promises of God over your life. As you pray, reflect on your identity in Christ, and recommit any place in your life that is needed to walk in a manner worthy of the calling you have received.

2. Pray for other leaders you know to stand against the lies and schemes of the enemy that are set against them, that God would strengthen them and give them true identity.

3. Pray that those in your church or small-group community would live a life worthy of our collective calling and fulfill the assignment God has given us.

Family Moment: Walking worthy

Read Colossians 1:9-14. Make a family foot collage. Using washable paint, stamp the bottom of one foot of each person in your family onto a separate sheet of paper, or trace each person's foot with a marker. When the footprints have dried, cut each piece out and glue them so they overlap onto an 11x17 sheet of paper. Notice the difference in sizes—we are each at a different stage of life and in our walk with Christ. Write the following on the collage: "We choose to walk worthy of the Lord. We will grow to know Him more."

Steps toward spiritual *maturity* are achieved through daily dependence, faith, surrender and obedience *toward* God.

Days 07 through **09**

Day 07 —— On our knees

Let's posture ourselves to give up anything that is keeping us from God's presence.

Today's Scripture

"For this reason I bow my knees to the Father of our Lord Jesus Christ, from whom the whole family in heaven and earth is named, that He would grant you, according to the riches of His glory, to be strengthened with might through His Spirit in the inner man, that Christ may dwell in your hearts through faith; that you, being rooted and grounded in love, may be able to comprehend with all the saints what is the width and length and depth and height—to know the love of Christ which passes knowledge; that you may be filled with all the fullness of God. Now to Him who is able to do exceedingly abundantly above all that we ask or think, according to the power that works in us, to Him be glory in the church by Christ Jesus to all generations, forever and ever. Amen."
—Ephesians 3:14-21 (NKJV)

Reflect on the Word

At its foundation, Paul is desperate for one thing: that every part of God would come to live in every part of us, to be totally filled up by God's presence without friction or empty space. This makes the first line imperative: "I bow my knees to the Father." The way to be filled with God is to be emptied of self. The way to receive His strength is to lay down our own. The more we daily surrender our lives, the more fully we come to experience His.

Prayer + Contemplation

1. Reread and reflect on each phrase from this prayer found in Ephesians. Which ones is God highlighting for further contemplation?

2. What do you need to lay down today to receive the fullness of God? If you're able to, kneel or lie down as you pray in a posture of humility.

3. Pray for the Holy Spirit to reveal what parts of your life you are holding onto and then trade them in to receive the fullness of God's love there.

Family Moment: Speak a blessing

Read **Ephesians 3:14-21**. What stands out to you in these verses? Take turns praying a blessing over each family member by name: "May God strengthen [name] with power through His Holy Spirit in your inner being. We pray that you will have the power to grasp how wide and long and high and deep the love of Jesus is for you. May you be filled to the measure of all the fullness of God and know that He is able to do more than we can ask or imagine. Amen."

Day 08 —— He is our deliverance

God is faithful, and His protection is our strength.

Today's Scripture

"As for other matters, brothers and sisters, pray for us that the message of the Lord may spread rapidly and be honored, just as it was with you. And pray that we may be delivered from wicked and evil people, for not everyone has faith. But the Lord is faithful, and He will strengthen you and protect you from the evil one. We have confidence in the Lord that you are doing and will continue to do the things we command. May the Lord direct your hearts into God's love and Christ's perseverance."
—2 Thessalonians 3:1-5 (NIV)

Additional Scripture
Ephesians 6:12 (NKJV)

Reflect on the Word

It is God's job to deliver us. It is our job to pray and ask for it. And though Paul asks for deliverance from wicked people, he says the Lord will protect us from the evil one. This is a reminder our protection is not against flesh and blood—not even the flesh and blood of evil people—but the principalities and powers at work within them (Eph. 6:12). And God will protect us. But He will first strengthen us. So, when deliverance seems to tarry, trust that the pressure is directing you into God's love and forming Jesus' perseverance within you.

Prayer + Contemplation

1. Where are you taking deliverance and protection into your own hands instead of trusting in God to bring it about in His timing? Confess and place it in God's hands.

2. Are there people about whom God needs to remind you that your battle is not with them? Pray to see them as God sees them, and pray for their deliverance and protection, too.

3. Pray to trust God as your deliverer, even amid painful trials and tribulations.

Family Moment: Power of prayer

Read 2 Thessalonians 3:1-5. Prayer is powerful! In Paul's letter to the Thessalonians, he asks them to pray. Prayer is our greatest weapon against the enemy. We too have the assignment to pray God's protection over others in His power. Write "God is our protector" on a piece of paper. Around that truth, write names of people you know in need of God's protection. Maybe they are staff members from your church, people at school, family members or neighbors. Take turns praying for the people on your new "prayer board." If helpful, use the following prayer for each name: "Lord, please be faithful to strengthen and protect [name] from the evil one."

Notes

Day 09 —— Our first calling

If we focus on simply being with Jesus, His power, wisdom and revelation will be present in our lives.

Today's Scripture

"I keep asking that the God of our Lord Jesus Christ, the glorious Father, may give you the Spirit of wisdom and revelation, so that you may know Him better. I pray that the eyes of your heart may be enlightened in order that you may know the hope to which He has called you, the riches of His glorious inheritance in His holy people and His incomparably great power for us who believe. That power is the same as the mighty strength He exerted when He raised Christ from the dead and seated Him at His right hand in the heavenly realms, far above all rule and authority, power and dominion, and every name that is invoked, not only in the present age but also in the one to come. And God placed all things under His feet and appointed Him to be head over everything for the church, which is His body, the fullness of Him who fills everything in every way."
—Ephesians 1:17-23 (NIV)

Reflect on the Word

When Jesus named his 12 disciples, they were called to be with Him, to preach the gospel and to cast out demons. We often focus on the latter two callings, exciting as they are, and miss their source in the first—just being with Him. Ephesians tells us we can experience the same power that raised Jesus from the dead! It is the Holy Spirit who allows you to access this power, so that you may know Him better. To know Jesus is our first calling. All wisdom, revelation and power flow from our obedience to it.

Prayer + Contemplation

1. In what ways have you neglected your first calling to be with Jesus as you do ministry? Confess and repent.

2. Don't feel shame; we all fall short. Pray and ask Jesus for the courage to just be with Him without fear or agenda.

3. Pray for the Spirit of wisdom and revelation to be present in the church, that we might fulfill our first calling to simply be with Jesus and know Him better. Think about how to do that practically in worship.

Family Moment: Going deeper

Read **Ephesians 1:17-23**. As disciples of Jesus, our goal is to get to know Him better and deeper every single day! What are ways we can spend time with Jesus? Brainstorm together. Today we're going to respond to the prayer: "May God give you the Spirit of wisdom and revelation, so that you may know Him better." After praying, encourage every family member to spend time asking God how He wants them to respond to the verse. Use paper and coloring supplies, play a worship song or even just remain silent in Him. Share with one another how you spent your time.

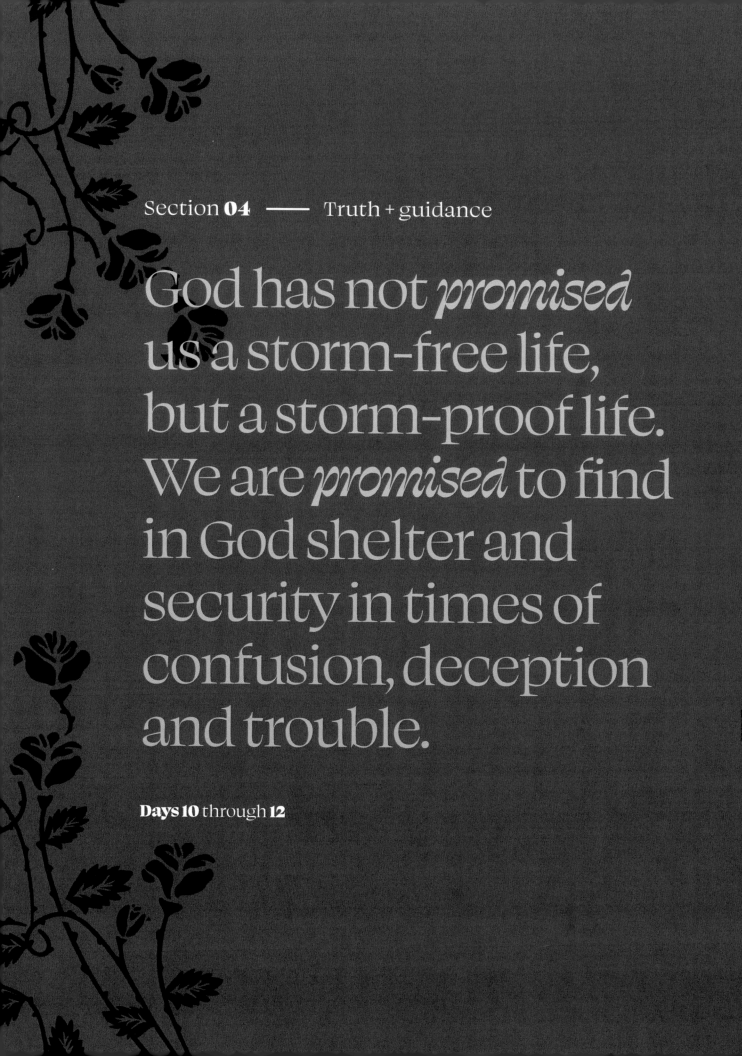

God has not *promised* us a storm-free life, but a storm-proof life. We are *promised* to find in God shelter and security in times of confusion, deception and trouble.

Days 10 through **12**

Day 10 — A solid foundation

God's Word promises us that even in the worst of times, He is our anchor.

Today's Scripture

"But mark this: There will be terrible times in the last days. People will be lovers of themselves, lovers of money, boastful, proud, abusive, disobedient to their parents, ungrateful, unholy, without love, unforgiving, slanderous, without self-control, brutal, not lovers of the good, treacherous, rash, conceited, lovers of pleasure rather than lovers of God—having a form of godliness but denying its power. Have nothing to do with such people."
—2 Timothy 3:1-5 (NIV)

"But as for you, continue in what you have learned and have become convinced of, because you know those from whom you learned it, and how from infancy you have known the Holy Scriptures, which are able to make you wise for salvation through faith in Christ Jesus. All Scripture is God-breathed and is useful for teaching, rebuking, correcting and training in righteousness, so that the servant of God may be thoroughly equipped for every good work."
—2 Timothy 3:14-17 (NIV)

Additional Scripture
Hebrews 4:12-13 (NIV)
Matthew 7:24-27 (NIV)

Reflect on the Word

Like a house with a solid foundation or a tree with a healthy root system, our lives can only withstand the turbulent shifting of the times when Christ is at the center of our life, faith and practice. God's Word has brought order out of chaos, calmed the wind and rain, and raised the dead to life; these same words of truth can anchor your life amid storms in whatever season you are facing.

Prayer + Contemplation

1. As you assess your life, what scriptures are you meditating on to keep you anchored in Christ through dark times?

2. Pray for those around you who are walking through a difficult season (e.g., health issues, relationships, finances, ministry). Ask God to give them encouragement and hope, that they would spend time in His Word and among His people.

3. Ask God to give His Word deep and lasting roots in your heart to keep you steady and stable in seasons of disruption and disorientation.

Family Moment: Time to build

Read Matthew 7:24-27. Gather some building supplies such as cards, blocks and marshmallows. Work as a family to construct houses, then test them by blowing air or shaking the table. Which ones survived? Which collapsed? Why do you think Jesus told the story in Matthew 7? What might it mean to build your house on the rock? Pray and ask the Holy Spirit to guide you and help you be obedient to God, even during difficult times.

Day 11 —— Shelter from the storms

In times of trouble, we must pray and take refuge "under His wings."

Today's Scripture

"He who dwells in the secret place of the Most High shall abide under the shadow of the Almighty. I will say of the Lord, 'He is my refuge and my fortress; my God, in Him I will trust.' Surely He shall deliver you from the snare of the fowler and from the perilous pestilence. He shall cover you with His feathers, and under His wings you shall take refuge; His truth shall be your shield and buckler. You shall not be afraid of the terror by night, nor of the arrow that flies by day, nor of the pestilence that walks in darkness, nor of the destruction that lays waste at noonday. A thousand may fall at your side, and ten thousand at your right hand; but it shall not come near you."
—Psalm 91:1-7 (NKJV)

Additional Scripture
Psalm 23:1-6 (NKJV)

Prayer + Contemplation

1. Consider and name areas in your life that incite fear, anxiety or worry; write them down. Now, pray and invite God, your Comforter and Protector, into each area.

2. Pray for those experiencing fear or anxiety, that they would experience peace from God that will surpass their current circumstances.

3. Lift up those living in imminent danger across the globe because of their faith in Jesus, that they would receive supernatural protection as they continue to proclaim Christ in their context.

Reflect on the Word

Tragedies, traumas and triggers consistently remind us of how unpredictable and dangerous the world can be. Yet, the Scriptures regularly point us back to God, whose care and compassion invite us to rest under the shadow of His wing and experience the presence and protection of the one who "never slumbers or sleeps" (**Ps. 121:4, NLT**). Though we experience difficult seasons, we do not have to fear that we face it alone because God is our "ever-present help in trouble" (**Ps. 46:1, NIV**).

Family Moment: Family fortress

Create a family fortress with pillows and blankets. Gather inside and discuss what everyone thinks about when they hear the word "refuge" and "fortress." Read **Psalm 91:1-7** together. What does it mean to say God is our "refuge" and "fortress"? Share examples of God's protection in your life and from the Bible. Is there something you're afraid of today? After sharing, invite everyone to speak God's Word over each fear shared: "God, You're my refuge. I trust in You, and I'm safe!"

Notes

_____
_____
_____
_____
_____
_____
_____
_____
_____
_____
_____
_____
_____
_____
_____
_____
_____
_____

Day 12 —— Hear His voice

Prayer is the key to filtering the voice of God from all other distractions and enabling us to hear Him.

Today's Scripture

"Trust in the Lord with all your heart and lean not on your own understanding; in all your ways submit to Him, and He will make your paths straight. Do not be wise in your own eyes; fear the Lord and shun evil. This will bring health to your body and nourishment to your bones. Honor the Lord with your wealth, with the first fruits of all your crops; then your barns will be filled to overflowing, and your vats will brim over with new wine. My son, do not despise the Lord's discipline, and do not resent His rebuke, because the Lord disciplines those He loves, as a father the son He delights in. Blessed are those who find wisdom, those who gain understanding."
—Proverbs 3:5-13 (NIV)

Additional Scripture
Psalm 25:4-5 (NIV)

Reflect on the Word

In a world where information is readily available, it is important to consider what voices guide our lives. A simple internet search might help us prove anything we think is right. God's voice may not shout at us like pop-up banner ads, but He is always available to guide us in wisdom, anchor us in truth and correct us when we are wrong. As we trust the Lord with our whole lives, we can be confident that we are being cared for and led toward God's best for us.

Prayer + Contemplation

1. Consider what voices get most of your attention and guide your life (e.g., pastors, politicians, influencers, authors, mentors, teachers, family members). How might you make more room for God's voice in your everyday life?

2. Pray for those who feel far from God, unsure of their call and lacking purpose. If someone comes to mind, pray that they would hear and respond to God's voice inviting them to trust and recenter their lives in Him.

3. Pray that God will illuminate the places in your life that need to be submitted (or resubmitted) to His lordship and guidance.

Family Moment: God is our guide

Read Psalm 25:4-5. Listening to Jesus can be difficult with all the distractions in our daily lives. Adults, choose a simple message (e.g., "We pray for God to protect you every single day."). Have one parent read the message in a low voice while the rest of the family shouts contradictory messages, makes noises and creates as much distraction as possible. See how hard it is to hear that one voice in the chaos? Now whisper the message into another's ear while everyone is quiet. That's how prayer can work! Life will be full of chaos and distractions, and it's so important we keep our eyes and ears open to Him every day.

Believers often face spiritual conflict and opposition. However, *in Christ*, we are given all we need to walk in the *authority* and *victory* Jesus purchased for us in His death and resurrection.

Days 13 through **15**

Day 13 — The armor of God

Withstanding spiritual opposition requires our responsive, conscious action.

Today's Scripture

"Finally, be strong in the Lord and in His mighty power. Put on the full armor of God, so that you can take your stand against the devil's schemes. For our struggle is not against flesh and blood, but against the rulers, against the authorities, against the powers of this dark world and against the spiritual forces of evil in the heavenly realms. Therefore put on the full armor of God, so that when the day of evil comes, you may be able to stand your ground, and after you have done everything, to stand. Stand firm then, with the belt of truth buckled around your waist, with the breastplate of righteousness in place, and with your feet fitted with the readiness that comes from the gospel of peace. In addition to all this, take up the shield of faith, with which you can extinguish all the flaming arrows of the evil one. Take the helmet of salvation and the sword of the Spirit, which is the word of God. And pray in the Spirit on all occasions with all kinds of prayers and requests. With this in mind, be alert and always keep on praying for all the Lord's people."
—Ephesians 6:10-18 (NIV)

Reflect on the Word

As believers, we know that spiritual forces are behind many of the battles we face. Our preparation and strength to overcome such evil are abundantly provided by the Lord of heaven's army. His protection and resources are great, intended for the individual believer and the collective church. Withstanding spiritual opposition requires our responsive, conscious action. Let us put on, take up, stand firm, be alert and pray unceasingly in the Spirit, walking in the victory He has already secured on our behalf.

Prayer + Contemplation

1. Consider God's personal and corporate call to battle readiness and the divine protection of spiritual armor He generously supplies. Write down some ways God has protected you in the past.

2. Pray in the Spirit for friends and family facing battles of many kinds, that they would be strengthened, protected and comforted by God's presence and heavenly provision.

3. Clothed in the armor of God, and with the authority of the indwelling Holy Spirit, bind the enemy that prowls around seeking to devour, and declare the goodness of God over your life and circumstances.

Family Moment: The armor of God

Read Ephesians 6:10-18. Gather the following supplies for armor of God dress up: belt, coat (breastplate), shoes, plate (shield), bike helmet and paper-towel tube (or toy sword). Select a family member to put on all the items as someone reads this passage out loud. Name the items as you put them on, and have kids shout out what they stand for (e.g., "Belt?" "Truth!"). The armor of God reminds us that God fights for us, and He equips us with everything we need to stand firm. Talk about the "battles" you faced last week (big or small), and discuss how the armor of God would be helpful for each battle shared.

Let's celebrate Jesus' atonement and victory on the cross, and the righteousness He offers us.

Today's Scripture

"When you were dead in your sins and in the uncircumcision of your flesh, God made you alive with Christ. He forgave us all our sins, having canceled the charge of our legal indebtedness, which stood against us and condemned us; He has taken it away, nailing it to the cross. And having disarmed the powers and authorities, He made a public spectacle of them, triumphing over them by the cross."
—Colossians 2:13-15 (NIV)

Additional Scripture
Revelation 12:10-11 (NKJV)

Prayer + Contemplation

1. Pause, breathe and contemplate the reality of Christ's fulfillment of the law, your identification with Him, and the resulting victory over the powers of darkness.

2. Contend for loved ones who are seeking righteousness by their own strength, that they would recognize and receive that which was already accomplished through the cross.

3. Ask the Holy Spirit to illuminate ways you rely on self-sufficiency or lean into legalism, and allow Him to bring corrective healing to those areas.

Reflect on the Word

It is finished! In Jesus, the law is satisfied, our debt is paid, and the enemy of our soul is defeated. All strivings cease through the victory of the cross. Our confession of faith and identification with Christ clothes us in His righteousness, setting us free from the accuser. We are liberated by the blood of Jesus under the authority of God's Word, empowered to overcome the dark forces of this world.

Family Moment: Righteous in Christ

Read **Colossians 2:13-14**. What does the word "righteous" mean?* Because God is righteous, He cannot tolerate sin. But God is also loving. Because of His love for us, He makes a way for us to be free from sin and brings us back into His family. Jesus takes our sin and gives us His righteousness. Through Jesus, we not only can live in God's presence, but God's Holy Spirit lives in us to help us to become like God. This is the Good News! Have you made the decision to follow Jesus? Adults, share your testimony with your children, and offer them the opportunity to follow Jesus, or celebrate with them if they already are.

*Answer: The word "righteous" means perfect, holy, without sin.

Day 15 —— Authority in prayer

As children of God, we have been given authority over the enemy's snares; let's grasp it!

Today's Scripture

"He replied, 'I saw Satan fall like lightning from heaven. I have given you authority to trample on snakes and scorpions and to overcome all the power of the enemy; nothing will harm you. However, do not rejoice that the spirits submit to you, but rejoice that your names are written in heaven.'"
—Luke 10:18-20 (NIV)

Prayer + Contemplation

1. Allow the joy of your salvation and the understanding of Christ's headship over all things to be the strength of your warfare.

2. Intercede on behalf of someone you know who is far from God, that they might recognize the spiritual battle and come to understand the power and authority of Christ.

3. Ask for revelation of what's behind any opposition you're presently facing, take authority over the enemy, and release the promises of God over that situation.

"I pray that the eyes of your heart may be enlightened in order that you may know the hope to which He has called you, the riches of His glorious inheritance in His holy people, and His incomparably great power for us who believe. That power is the same as the mighty strength He exerted when He raised Christ from the dead and seated Him at his right hand in the heavenly realms, far above all rule and authority, power and dominion, and every name that is invoked, not only in the present age but also in the one to come. And God placed all things under His feet and appointed Him to be head over everything for the church, which is His body, the fullness of Him who fills everything in every way."
—Ephesians 1:18-23 (NIV)

Reflect on the Word

As overcomers in faith and as children of God, we are to rejoice and fear not! We walk, pray and live as co-heirs (with Christ) who have been given all power and authority over the enemy with the knowledge that our eternity is secure. In the authoritative name of Jesus, our fervent prayers of agreement are powerful and effective, with assurance that what we bind and loose on Earth will be bound and loosed in heaven.

Family Moment: Promise prayers

Read Ephesians 1:18-23. Share the words that stand out to you. God invites us to pray big prayers with the power and authority that comes from following Jesus. What does it mean to pray with authority? Declaring the promises of God is a great place to start. Go on a promise hunt through the Bible, e.g., He loves you (Rom. 5:8), He hears you (Ps. 34:17), You are His child (John 1:12), and He will never leave you (Deut. 31:8). Invite everyone to find a promise of God.

Notes

We belong to Jesus, and by our life in Him, we are the *ecclesia*—the embodied *presence* of Jesus in this world. We are *called out* of this world and into a new community called the church.

Days 16 through **18**

To all the saints in Christ Jesus who
...hilippi, with the overseers and dea...
...u and peace from God our Father...
...Christ. I thank my God in all
...ce of you, always in eve...
...making my prayer
...rtnership in the...

...pray for t...
who will believe in...
...they all may be on...
...l in You; that the...
world may believ...
...ory which You...
...y may be o...
...in Me; th...
...at the...
...d hav...

...handami...
...n los unos a l...
...mado, tambié...
...os unos a los o...
...todos sabrán qu...
...scipulos, si se ama...

...Y a dónde vas, S...
...n Pedro,
...espondió:
...de yo voy, no p...
...me seguirá...
...insistió Pe...
...irte ahora?

Day 16 —— In it for the long haul

How can you make an impact in your relationships and mission?

Today's Scripture

"The "Paul and Timothy, bondservants of Jesus Christ, to all the saints in Christ Jesus who are at Philippi, with the bishops and deacons: grace to you and peace from God our Father and the Lord Jesus Christ. I thank my God upon every remembrance of you, always in every prayer of mine making request for you all with joy, for your fellowship in the gospel from the first day until now, being confident of this very thing, that He who has begun a good work in you will complete it until the day of Jesus Christ; just as it is right for me to think this of you all, because I have you in my heart, inasmuch as both in my chains and in the defense and confirmation of the gospel, you all are partakers with me of grace. For God is my witness, how greatly I long for you all with the affection of Jesus Christ. And this I pray, that your love may abound still more and more in knowledge and all discernment, that you may approve the things that are excellent, that you may be sincere and without offense till the day of Christ, being filled with the fruits of righteousness which are by Jesus Christ, to the glory and praise of God."
—Philippians 1:1-11 (NKJV)

Reflect on the Word

Every time Paul prays for the Philippians, it's a prayer of thanks and joy. His gratefulness is because of their partnership in the gospel that remained throughout the years. Do you see? Steadfast love produces joy. The Philippians loved Paul well by partnering with him in the gospel over time. They didn't pitch in just for a season, but they remained by his side for the long haul. We are called to this type of partnership. When you look at the relationships that have the greatest impact on others, it is the ones in which people love each other faithfully in all seasons of life.

Prayer + Contemplation

1. We need one another to accomplish God's mission together. Make a list of those who make up the ecclesia, the embodied presence of Jesus in this world, around you.

2. Pray for Christians to long for one another with the affection of Christ Jesus.

3. Ask God to create faithful partnerships in your life like Paul had with the church of Philippi.

Family Moment: Thank you cards

Read Philippians 1:1-11. What stands out to you in Paul's prayer for the Philippians? Think about who God has placed in your life to encourage you and help you be more like Jesus. This could be someone at church, a friend or even someone in your family. Draw or write a card for this person (or people!) telling them how thankful you are for them. You may even want to include a verse from Philippians 1.

Notes

Day 17 —— Unity in love

We, the body of Christ, are called to love one another in spite of our imperfections.

Today's Scripture

"I do not pray for these alone, but also for those who will believe in Me through their word; that they all may be one, as You, Father, are in Me, and I in You; that they also may be one in Us, that the world may believe that You sent Me. And the glory which You gave Me I have given them, that they may be one just as We are one: I in them, and You in Me; that they may be made perfect in one, and that the world may know that You have sent Me, and have loved them as You have loved Me."
—John 17:20-23 (NKJV)

"A new commandment I give to you, that you love one another; as I have loved you, that you also love one another. By this all will know that you are My disciples, if you have love for one another."
—John 13:34-35 (NKJV)

Reflect on the Word

Have you heard the expression, "I like Jesus, but not the church"? This sentiment grieves the heart of Jesus because Jesus loves His church. He loves the broken, faulty, work-in-progress church. He allowed himself to be humiliated, beaten and murdered for it. He patiently loves His bride. In the same manner, He desires us to walk in unity, loving one another as He has loved us—even in the midst of this broken, faulty, work-in-progress world. Together, we can be grateful that God uses even our imperfections to reveal Himself to a world in need of His perfect love.

Prayer + Contemplation

1. Jesus wants His disciples to live in such a way that the work of God is evident in them. How can you do this practically, every day?

2. Pray for an outpouring of God's unconditional love upon the church, so that we may be made complete and full as one.

3. Ask God to help you develop relationships with people from other cultures as well as to create opportunity for cross-cultural fellowship.

Family Moment: Unity sculptures

Read John 13:34-35. As followers of Jesus, we're unified through God's Spirit. Why is it sometimes hard to be unified with others? God knows it's hard for us to get along with other people sometimes. Thankfully we have the gift and the power of the Holy Spirit to help us love all people, even when it's hard. Practice unity as a family by gathering some modeling clay or dough and straws, and construct a creative sculpture where everyone builds an important part and all parts fit together. As you work, brainstorm ways your family can show God's love to others in the week ahead.

Notes

Day 18 —— Interdependence day

As believers, we are in the world together as the body of Christ; let's use our gifts for His glory.

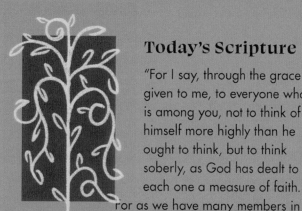

Today's Scripture

"For I say, through the grace given to me, to everyone who is among you, not to think of himself more highly than he ought to think, but to think soberly, as God has dealt to each one a measure of faith. For as we have many members in one body, but all the members do not have the same function, so we, being many, are one body in Christ, and individually members of one another. Having then gifts differing according to the grace that is given to us, let us use them: if prophecy, let us prophesy in proportion to our faith; or ministry, let us use it in our ministering; he who teaches, in teaching; he who exhorts, in exhortation; he who gives, with liberality; he who leads, with diligence; he who shows mercy, with cheerfulness."
—Romans 12:3-8 (NKJV)

Additional Scripture
Romans 12:9-16 (NKJV)
1 Corinthians 12:12-14, 25-27 (NKJV)

Reflect on the Word

God loves diversity, yet He calls us to be one. There is no such thing as private Christianity. As Jesus' body, if one part suffers, all the parts suffer with it. We should share one another's burdens in other to help lighten them. Likewise, if one part is honored, all the parts are glad. Believers need to be able to empathize with others, to join in their struggles as if they themselves were experiencing them. They should suffer with others, offering kindness, concern, compassion and a shoulder to cry on when needed.

Prayer + Contemplation

1. Let us be kind to one another with brotherly love and honor. Pray and ask who you need to offer extra kindness to this week. Write their name down, and ask God to show you how to bring them supernatural kindness.

2. Pray for God to remove selfish behavior from the body of Christ.

3. Ask the Holy Spirit to perfect us in our oneness with Jesus.

Family Moment:
The body of Christ

Read Romans 12:3-8. The body of Christ is an amazing part of God's plan to bless the world. What gift has God given you that you might use to bring unity to your community? Write down one or two things each family member can do this week, and make a plan to bless others. End the time by speaking a blessing over everyone in your family: "Now we are the body of Christ, and each of us is a part of it! Holy Spirit, please give us power to serve others with the gifts we've been given."

Notes

Jesus has given us the *Great Commission,* and we do this in the power of His *Spirit* and the promise of His abiding *presence.*

Days 19 through **21**

Day 19 —— Spirit-filled boldness

Only by the infilling of the Holy Spirit can we preach and go with boldness and the strength of God.

Today's Scripture

"So when the apostles were with Jesus, they kept asking him, 'Lord, has the time come for you to free Israel and restore our kingdom?' He replied, 'The Father alone has the authority to set those dates and times, and they are not for you to know. But you will receive power when the Holy Spirit comes upon you. And you will be my witnesses, telling people about me everywhere—in Jerusalem, throughout Judea, in Samaria and to the ends of the earth.'"
—Acts 1:6-8 (NLT)

Additional Scripture
Acts 4:23-31 (NLT)

Prayer + Contemplation

1. Am I actively discerning what God is doing in this time and season (versus passively watching world events) and taking steps of faith to join Him in new kingdom endeavors?

2. Pause. (No, really—pause right now.) Open yourself up to a fresh infilling of living power from the Spirit to equip you with gifts and boldness for your next opportunity to be a living witness of the living Savior.

3. Since "everywhere" is a very big space, ask God for timely discernment for your specific assignment to be in the right place at the right time doing the right things for the advance of His kingdom.

Reflect on the Word

When our confidence to speak about Jesus is challenged, we have a remedy to hesitation. Prayer creates immunity to intimidation and deeply connects us to God's great mission. When tempted toward restraint, the power of the Spirit is expansive, opening our mouths to speak, moving our feet to go. The prayers of the early church pivoted them from uncertainty to unstoppable boldness. Scripture-informed prayer quiets confusion, provokes courage and initiates fresh infillings of God's Spirit.

Family Moment: In His strength

Read Acts 4:23-31. Just as the disciples were filled with the Holy Spirit, we followers of Jesus are filled with the Holy Spirit. God is powerful, and He gives us the strength to follow Jesus and tell others about Him. Share about a time you experienced God's power. Next, gather a piece of paper and pen to create a list of things you've been trying to do in your own strength. It could be tasks at work or school, trying to make a friend or even manual tasks. After sharing, surrender your list to God in prayer: "God, we're tired of doing it on our own. Please help us give all these things to Your Spirit, and fill us with Your power."

Notes

_____
_____
_____
_____
_____
_____
_____
_____
_____
_____
_____
_____
_____
_____
_____
_____
_____
_____
_____

Jesus' encouragement for us to pray and ask helps us grow in faith and on mission.

Today's Scripture

"Continue earnestly in prayer, being vigilant in it with thanksgiving; meanwhile praying also for us, that God would open to us a door for the Word, to speak the mystery of Christ, for which I am also in chains, that I may make it manifest, as I ought to speak. Walk in wisdom toward those who are outside, redeeming the time. Let your speech always be with grace, seasoned with salt, that you may know how you ought to answer each one."
—Colossians 4:2-6 (NKJV)

"Ask, and it will be given to you; seek, and you will find; knock, and it will be opened to you. For everyone who asks receives, and he who seeks finds, and to him who knocks it will be opened."
—Matthew 7:7-8 (NKJV)

Reflect on the Word

In Colossians 4, Paul provides ingredients for sustained prayer, followed by a heartfelt request to speak boldly—Being chained does not prevent open doors!—and a call to redemptive living and speech. Next consider the words of Jesus in Matthew 7:7-8. His clear, simple and certain promise of a response to our asking, seeking and knocking is faith-enlarging. Tap into the immeasurable results of specific prayer today.

Prayer + Contemplation

1. As we near the close of 21 days of intentional prayer and fasting, how has your heart been changed through this daily time of prayer? How can you retain this habit going forward?

2. Partner with God and ask for Him to strengthen your practices of prayer and devotion, to add any missing ingredients and to continuously overflow and energize you.

3. God opens doors for those who persist in prayer. Bring what seems locked and closed to Him now, asking humbly for openings and answers.

Family Moment: Prayer walk

Read **Matthew 7:7-8**. The Bible teaches us to pray often—without ceasing, even! Why do you think Jesus shared these words? God wants to open the doors and give us the things we pray and ask for. Take time as a family to go outdoors on a prayer walk (or a prayer drive, if the weather isn't cooperating). While you are out, take turns praying for your neighborhood, school and church. Look around for people or places over whom you can pray. Consider bringing a prayer journal along to remember the prayer requests.

Notes

Page 57

Notes

Page 57

Day *21* —— Strength to soar

Reflect on the blessing and lessons of 21 focused days of prayer, and prepare for a future on mission with God.

Today's Scripture

"We also pray that you will be strengthened with all his glorious power so you will have all the endurance and patience you need. May you be filled with joy, always thanking the Father. He has enabled you to share in the inheritance that belongs to His people, who live in the light. For He has rescued us from the kingdom of darkness and transferred us into the Kingdom of His dear Son, who purchased our freedom and forgave our sins."
—Colossians 1:11-14 (NLT)

Additional Scripture
Isaiah 40:28-31 (NKJV)
Galatians 6:8-10 (NIV)

Prayer + Contemplation

1. Cultivate vision and expectation that God is doing great things in and through you, things beyond all you can ask, think or imagine! Write down the dreams God is giving you, and remember to pray about them often.

2. Pray your way into the great promises of these passages and receive endurance, patience, joy, a glorious inheritance, the harvest of doing good and renewed strength to soar.

3. Ask for and receive spiritual sight and eternal perspective along with divine resources to rise above your earthly circumstances, especially the things that wear you down.

Reflect on the Word

Today, as we conclude our 21 days together, receive the strength you lack so you can enter the inheritance you don't deserve. Welcome His glorious power and renewed confidence to enjoy the riches appointed for all who are rescued, ransomed, forgiven and adopted by the Father. Why languish on the outskirts of abundance when you are invited into overflowing life? Don't give up on the promise of sowing and reaping good. Press on, weary one, you are appointed for blessing!

Family Moment: Blessed by prayer

Read **Colossians 1:11-14**. We pray your 21 days together was filled with new conversations and Holy Spirit "Aha!" moments. To conclude your 21 days, share sightings of God from the journey. What did He reveal to you? How did you see Him at work? How did you see Him at work in someone in your family? Share reflections and responses before ending with a blessing. Pray over each family member: "[Name], we pray you will be strengthened with God's power. May you be filled with joy, always thanking God, for He has rescued you from the kingdom of darkness and transferred you into the kingdom of His son, who purchased our freedom and forgave our sins."

A word of *thanks*

Thank you for joining us for 21 Days of Prayer + Fasting 2024. Our greatest desire is that you grew as a family, united on mission, and learned from one another, as well. A special thanks goes out to everyone who worked on and prayed over this devotional. We hope the last 21 days have been a blessing, and that your family will continue together in prayer and fellowship.

The **21 Days of Prayer + Fasting 2024** *team*

Editors
Marcia Graham
Amanda Borowski
Bill Shepson
Lindsay Willis

Content + Project Coordination
Erin Edquist
Cheryl Johnson
Jordan McKenna

Spanish Translation + Coordination
Diana Edwards
Raul Irigoyen
Rebekka Otremba
Melisa Prieto

Design
Josh Hernandez
PJ Moon

Website
Ben Gurrad

Video
Caique Morais

Social Media
Luke La Vine

Special thanks to our writers + contributors:
George B., Eduardo Bogea, Katie Gale, Nicole Hill, Benji
Horning, Tami Jones, Russell Joyce, Phil Maginelli, Wendy
Nolasco, Randy Remington, Jennifer Thigpenn, Ted Vail,
Caleb Valdovinos

Made in the USA
Las Vegas, NV
10 January 2024

84162409R00038